MIDLOTHIAN PUBLIC LIBRARY

3 1614 00165 7007

P9-CAR-549

MIDLOTHIAN
PUBLIC LIBRARY

BAKER & TAYLOR

Mardi Gras

ABDO
Publishing Company

A Buddy Book
by
Julie Murray

MIDLOTHIAN PUBLIC LIBRARY
14701 S. KENTON AVE.
MIDLOTHIAN, IL 60445

Buddy BOOKS
Holidays

VISIT US AT
www.abdopublishing.com

Published by ABDO Publishing Company, PO Box 398166, Minneapolis, Minnesota 55439.

Copyright © 2014 by Abdo Consulting Group, Inc. International copyrights reserved in all countries. No part of this book may be reproduced in any form without written permission from the publisher. Buddy Books™ is a trademark and logo of ABDO Publishing Company.

Printed in the United States of America, North Mankato, Minnesota.
092013
012014

 PRINTED ON RECYCLED PAPER

Coordinating Series Editor: Rochelle Baltzer
Editor: Sarah Tieck
Contributing Editors: Megan M. Gunderson, Bridget O'Brien, Marcia Zappa
Graphic Design: Denise Esner
Cover Photograph: *AP Photo*: Photo/Northwest Florida Daily News, Devon Ravine.
Interior Photographs/Illustrations: *AP Photo*: Hassan Ammar (p. 22), Alex Brandon (p. 15), News-Gazette, John Dixon (p. 6), Bill Haber (p. 5), Gerald Herbert (p. 15), Mark Humphrey (p. 21), Louisiana State Museum (p. 13), North Wind Picture Archives via AP Images (p. 11), Charlie Varley / Sipa USA (Sipa via AP Images) (p. 17); *iStockphoto*: ©iStockphoto.com/dswebb (p. 17); *Shutterstock*: DeliriumTrigger (p. 19), margouillat photo (p. 9), Pixelbliss (p. 7), RoJo Images (p. 19).

Library of Congress Cataloging-in-Publication Data

Murray, Julie, 1969-
  Mardi Gras / Julie Murray.
    pages cm. -- (Holidays)
  ISBN 978-1-62403-186-1
1. Carnival--Juvenile literature. 2. Carnival--United States--Juvenile literature. 3. New Orleans (La.)--Social life and customs--Juvenile literature. I. Title.
  GT4180.M87 2014
  394.25--dc23
                          2013028916

Table of Contents

What Is Mardi Gras?

Mardi Gras (MAHR-dee grah) is **celebrated** around the world. It is a time when people attend parades, eat large meals, and have fun!

Mardi Gras is on a Tuesday between February 2 and March 9. It happens about 40 days before Easter. Mardi Gras may be celebrated for several days.

New Orleans, Louisiana, is known for its large Mardi Gras festival.

The Season of Lent

   Mardi Gras is the day before Ash Wednesday, which marks the beginning of Lent. Lent is 40 days. During this time, **Christians** pray and prepare for Easter.

At Ash Wednesday services, Christians have ash crosses made on their foreheads.

Years ago, people did not eat certain foods during Lent. So, they would eat all their extra meat, eggs, milk, and cheese before Lent. Today, people still have rules about what to eat during Lent.

Today, many people do not eat certain meats on special days during Lent. Many choose fish instead.

The Story of Mardi Gras

Mardi Gras got its start thousands of years ago. At that time, it was a spring **celebration**.

Later, it became a **Christian** tradition. During the **Middle Ages** in Europe, it became known as Shrove Tuesday. *Shrove* refers to the telling of sins.

Lent was a serious time. So on Shrove Tuesday, people wanted to have fun before it began!

People ate pancakes on Shrove Tuesday. These helped use up eggs and fat, which were not allowed during Lent.

First American Mardi Gras

Mardi Gras is French for "Fat Tuesday." Some historians believe the first American Mardi Gras was held on March 3, 1699. French explorers **celebrated** near what is now New Orleans, Louisiana.

As time went on, the celebration grew. Soon, there were street parties, costumed balls, and big meals. The first Mardi Gras parade was held in the late 1830s.

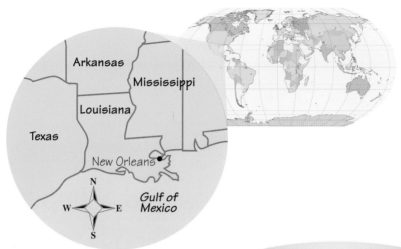

The French Quarter is a very old part of New Orleans. Many Mardi Gras parades have taken place there.

In 1857, there was a **torchlit** parade. It had floats and marching bands. It was organized by businessmen who called themselves the Mistick Krewe of Comus. Krewes are groups that put on parades and parties during Mardi Gras.

The Mistick Krewe of Comus was one of the first krewes. It is a secret group.

Parades

Today, New Orleans is famous for its Mardi Gras parades. Krewes still put on parades and parties. There are many different krewes.

The king of the **celebration** is called Rex. He is part of the Rex parade. The Rex Organization began in 1872. This famous group also chooses a queen and hosts a large party.

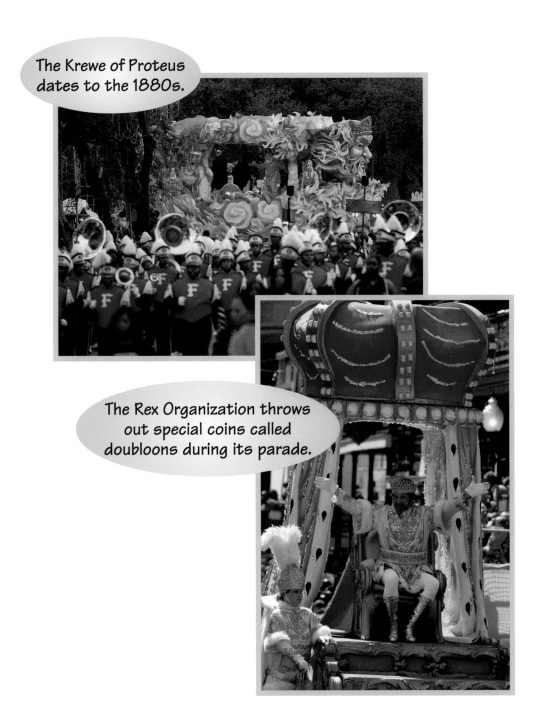

The Krewe of Proteus dates to the 1880s.

The Rex Organization throws out special coins called doubloons during its parade.

Throws

Masked people ride on floats in the city's parades. They toss small objects called "throws" for people to catch.

Popular throws include small toys, doubloons, and strings of beads. Many beads are purple, green, and gold. These colors **symbolize** justice, faith, and power.

Mardi Gras is famous for being a fun party! Many people dress up in costumes and beads.

King Cake

People eat king cake for Mardi Gras. A king cake is filled with cinnamon, fruit, or cream cheese.

A small toy baby is placed inside the cake. It **symbolizes** the baby Jesus, from **Christianity**. One person gets the piece of cake with the baby. He or she buys the next king cake or throws the next party.

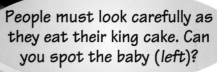

People must look carefully as they eat their king cake. Can you spot the baby (*left*)?

Mardi Gras Today

In the United States, Mardi Gras is a **legal** holiday in Louisiana. Other states have **celebrations**, too. These include Alabama and Mississippi. Mardi Gras is a time to celebrate and have fun!

The Mystic Krewe of Barkus has a dog parade! The costumes change with each year's parade theme.

Carnival

In many places around the world, the **celebration** before Lent is called Carnival. One famous celebration is in Rio de Janeiro, Brazil.

There, Carnival lasts for four days. Thousands of people travel to the city to have fun. They dance and listen to **samba** music.

In Rio de Janeiro, Carnival parades include lights and music.

Important Words

celebrate to observe a holiday with special events. These events are known as celebrations.

Christian (KRIHS-chuhn) a person who practices Christianity, which is a religion that follows the teachings of Jesus Christ.

legal based on or allowed by law.

Middle Ages a time in European history from about the 400s to the 1400s.

samba a Brazilian style of music and dance originally from Africa.

symbolize (SIHM-buh-lize) to serve as a symbol. A symbol is an object or mark that stands for an idea.

torchlit lighted by torches, which are burning sticks used to give light.

Web Sites

To learn more about Mardi Gras,

visit ABDO Publishing Company online. Web sites about Mardi Gras are featured on our Book Links page. These links are routinely monitored and updated to provide the most current information available.

www.abdopublishing.com

Index